Emotional Intelligence at School and Work

Stages of Emotional Development from Childhood to Adulthood for Greater Success in School, Work, and Life

Copyright © 2019 by Amanda M. Myers - All rights reserved.

The content contained within this book may not be reproduced, duplicated or transmitted without direct written permission from the author or the publisher.

Under no circumstances will any blame or legal responsibility be held against the publisher, or author, for any damages, reparation, or monetary loss due to the information contained within this book, either directly or indirectly.

Legal Notice:

This book is copyright protected. It is only for personal use. You cannot amend, distribute, sell, use, quote or paraphrase any part, or the content within this book, without the consent of the author or publisher.

Disclaimer Notice:

Please note the information contained within this document is for educational and entertainment purposes only. All effort has been executed to present accurate, up to date, reliable, complete information. No warranties of any kind are declared or implied. Readers acknowledge that the author is not engaging in the rendering of legal, financial, medical or professional advice. The content within this book has been derived from various sources. Please consult a licensed professional before attempting any techniques outlined in this book.

By reading this document, the reader agrees that under no circumstances is the author responsible for any losses, direct or indirect, that are incurred as a result of the use of information contained within this document, including, but not limited to, errors, omissions, or inaccuracies.

Table of Contents

Introduction	1
Chapter 1: Understanding Emotions	4
Chapter 2: What is Emotional Intelligence?	10
Chapter 3: Emotional Self-Regulation	15
Chapter 4: Self-Control of Negative Emotions	23
Chapter 5: Experiencing Emotions as a Student in School	31
Chapter 6: Experiencing Emotions as a Teacher or Parent	37
Chapter 7: Emotions Experienced in Childhood	48
Chapter 8: Emotions Experienced in Adolescence	54
Chapter 9: Emotions in Adulthood at the Workplace	62
Chapter 10: How to Manage Emotions in Your Career	71
Chapter 11: Emotional Regulation and Mental Health	80
Chapter 12: Maintaining Wellness Every Day	85
Conclusion	95
References	97

Introduction

Emotions color different aspects of our lives. In different ways, we are always experiencing feelings and thoughts that pass through our minds. At a given moment, we might be feeling and thinking about many different things at once. Our emotions are complex. We cannot put our finger on just one thing we are feeling. Sometimes, we feel a variety of things for different reasons. What is important is that we find ways of understanding our emotions at different phases of our lives. That is where this book comes in.

Emotional Intelligence (EQ) has become a hot topic in psychology and the self-help industry for the last several years. With Daniel Goleman's famous book "Emotional Intelligence" on the topic, it has been something that many doctors and therapists are teaching to their patients, so everyone can benefit from it. EQ has become more important than IQ and for many different reasons. Because EQ has garnered a lot of attention, many have acknowledged its importance in creating meaningful and fulfilling relationships.

In order to live a life full of good relationships, it is crucial to find ways of understanding not only our emotions, but those of our loved ones as well. If we can do that, then we can understand the humanity common to every one of us. We can empathize with others and cooperate to be productive individuals in the world today. Then, we can achieve the impossible and reach all of our objectives.

This book is about emotional intelligence and its presence in different stages of life. You may be a child, adolescent, or adult, but your emotions play into every phase of your life. Perhaps, you go to school or you are working to support your family. What is important to understand is how emotions develop at each phase of your life, so you can know how to respond to complex emotions. This book provides the answers to your questions about emotional intelligence at school and work. We will delve in to discover how people react emotionally at different life stages and in different environments. Using real-life-inspired examples and case studies, we will clearly illustrate and support the points we explain, so you have a broad picture of the world of emotional intelligence.

You may be wondering things like, "What am I feeling?", "Why do I feel that way?", "What is the best way to react emotionally to this situation?" We will explore strategies that you can reasonably and effectively use to deal with emotions whether you are young or old and in whatever life situation. We want to make this book relevant to all generations of readers. We know that you will find the material interesting, engaging, and meaningful, so you can fully understand your emotions and those of other people. Readers could include teachers, leaders, parents, among other people. Likewise, young readers can be invited to understand the emotions of others. We want everyone to be able to understand this important topic.

Thank you for purchasing this book. We know that you will enjoy reading about the topic of emotional intelligence and that it will provide valuable food for thought to help you live a thriving and more meaningful life. Read on to discover the world of emotions and your ways of successfully managing them.

Chapter 1:
Understanding Emotions

Deep down, we have emotions buried inside us. Sometimes, we choose to express our emotions freely and healthily. But at other times, we suppress our emotions and only let them out when they get out of hand, which can lead to both explosion and implosion. Our feelings are an important part of what makes us human beings.

Emotions provide the basis for our experience of the world. They provide an important pathway for how we act and behave in our lives. Often, we see that they impact us negatively through the violent expressions of them. We can fly off the handle easily if we are overcome with negative emotions. In addition, other people tend to influence us positively or negatively with their emotions, which is an important part of our lives. For example, when one person is feeling joyful and elated, other people will feel their positive energy and experience those feelings too. Conversely, if someone is negative, they will also feel the same way. This anger or frustration can deeply affect other people. A person who is constantly negative will create a hostile environment for others. For many years, psychologists have tried to study and understand emotions. One named Paul Ekman demonstrated that there are six basic types of emotions that are evident in people of all different cultures (Cherry, 2018). Let's look at the six basic emotions.

Happiness

Happiness is a feeling of elation, joy, peace, excitement, and exuberance, which is considered to be the most desirable emotion. A lot of research has been conducted on the topic, especially with the invention of positive psychology. Most of us desire to be happy in our lives. When we are happy, we show that we are relaxed, smiling, enjoying life, and benefiting from all the things of this life. Happiness includes positive body language and an upbeat voice that encourages everyone around a person (Cherry, 2018). Even though happiness is one of the most basic human emotions, it can easily become complicated by the trivial matters of this world, including money, power, success, and many other things. Many people add things such as having a big house, fancy car, or many possessions. These contribute to happiness, but are not essential parts of it.

Happiness is ultimately the desire of every human being. Everyone wants to live a meaningful and satisfying life, but very few people actually achieve it. Happiness that we experience is rooted in our identity and how we see ourselves. Feeling happy is an emotion that we feel inside of us, regardless of the external circumstances in which we find ourselves. Happiness has been shown to increase our longevity, improve our quality of life, reduce feelings of loneliness and isolation, and help us overcome depression.

Sadness

On the other end of the spectrum is sadness, which is shown in people who have a low mood state. This includes feelings of disappointment, grief, and mourning. We can experience sadness at different moments in our lives, including when we are feeling depressed. Sadness can either be a fleeting sensation or it can extend to long periods of spiritual depression. You can tell if a person is sad by their eyes which are downcast, or their tears as they cry. Sadness and depression can lead people to engage in unhealthy habits such as drinking, smoking, or simply cultivating a negative mindset. Such behaviors can become addictive and affect a person's life. Sadness has a lot of complexity to it, because it can come from a variety of sources (Cherry, 2018).

Surprise

Surprise is an emotion that requires a fight or flight response. Typically, when we are surprised, we are so overwhelmed with joy or fear that we lose control over ourselves. Surprise is a feeling that we have when something unexpected happens in our lives. Perhaps, it is hearing people sing, "Happy Birthday," as we walk through a door unexpectedly. We suddenly feel a shock to our system and think, "Wow, I'm so surprised." Our heart races and pounds as we see the smiling faces of our family and friends. Surprise is a fleeting emotion that lasts only a few seconds. You may feel it once but then afterward; other feelings may surface. Surprise is usually followed by feelings of disappointment and sadness or happiness and satisfaction. There are also unpleasant surprises that catch us off guard. For example, say you receive a bill in your mailbox for $2,000 in unpaid taxes. You may be shocked once you receive the news, but then you feel sad and depressed afterward when you consider how much you have to pay. It may also make you anxious and worried. Surprise is always followed by another emotion.

Anger

Anger is also a fight-or-flight response to given stimuli, wherein a person exhibits heightened emotion as a result of something that has offended or hurt them. When a person feels angry, they will have raised eyebrows, redness in the face, and have a threatening posture. Anger is something that can be sensed not just in the physical appearance of a person but also in their voice. Anger is an emotion that is not easily controlled and requires extensive experience to overcome. Many people are easily provoked to anger but they can learn how to control their anger and produce positive responses to their emotions (Cherry, 2018).

Disgust

Disgust is a combination emotion of surprise and disappointment. A person may be surprised to hear that one of the candidates of a recent election won. They were not expecting him to win, but he did. Not to mention any names, but there were more than a few people who were disappointed when Donald

Trump won the election. Once they heard, they felt both shocked and angry. This made them experience negative emotions. Disgust is something that is common to many different people, who have a negative emotional response to something they weren't expecting.

Fear

Fear is an emotion that we all feel when we think that we are in imminent danger or there is a threat. Think of seeing a deer run across the street. We might be scared out of our minds, because we see the animal come into our view and we feel that we might run over it. Fear is a fight-or-flight response that either causes us to run away from danger or fight it. When we see something horrible about to happen, we open our mouths and gasp. It is a natural emotion that we may experience each day.

Advanced Emotions

Many of our emotions are combinations of different emotions, and they affect how we behave. For example, we grieve when we experience loss, we experience surprise, sadness, and disappointment, among others. Grief manifests differently in different people. Combination emotions help us to understand how complex emotions can be. Often, we have to learn by experience how to name different emotions, so we can come up with the proper solutions to our problems.

Naming the Emotion

One of the most important things that you can do when dealing with your emotions is to name the emotion. Because emotions are complex, it can be difficult to pinpoint exactly what we're feeling at a given moment, but it is an important part of self-understanding. This helps a person move forward in their life.

Naming the emotion is a part of self-awareness, which is key to regulating your emotions. When you know how to identify what it is that you are feeling, you are more empowered to deal with your emotions. You feel more in control of your emotions. You no longer walk through life wondering how you can stop yourself from flying off the handle, because you know exactly what needs to get done.

Emotions are an important part of what makes us human. We may experience a lot of complex emotions, but we can be in full control of how we respond to those emotions. Emotional intelligence will teach you how you can be in full control of your feelings, so you respond in ways that will benefit you and your loved ones. We will show you how that works, as we look at the meaning of EQ and its implications for your life.

Chapter 2:
What is Emotional Intelligence?

Emotional intelligence is an important part of our daily lives. It is the ability to "perceive, control, and evaluate emotions" (Cherry, 2019). The term was made popular by Daniel Goleman. However, the term was first coined by a man named Michael Beloch in 1964 (Salazar, 2017). Emotional intelligence is a person's full awareness of their emotions and those of the people in their circles. It also includes the ability to distinguish between different kinds of emotions and respond appropriately to them. In order to fully understand emotional intelligence, certain models have been developed to explain it.

The Ability Model

Salovey and Mayer were the researchers who developed the Ability Model, which explains that emotional intelligence allows a person to improve their logical and critical thinking skills. This model mentions how a person's innate abilities allow them to understand emotions both within themselves and in the people around them. There are different skills a person may possess in emotional intelligence (Salazar, 2017).

Perceiving Emotions

The first skill is perceiving emotions. A person can understand the emotions within themselves and in other people. He or she can read the signs of an emotional response using both nonverbal and verbal communication.

Reasoning with Emotions

Secondly, a person can combine logical reasoning with emotions to solve everyday problems. They can also become more in tune with their surroundings.

Understanding Emotions

Thirdly, a person can understand the combination of emotions, which have different attributes and cause people to react differently. With this skill, a person recognizes the complexity of emotions and that emotions can respond to one another and form a colorful rainbow. Because everything is well-connected, one is able to understand the interactions with the emotions. For example, a person might go off on a tirade for being treated unfairly. Consequently, they would want to seek justice, retribution, or revenge for the act that had been committed against them (Salazar, 2017).

Management of emotions

Finally, the ability model includes the skill of managing emotions. A person will know how to self-regulate and respond appropriately to a wide range of situations in ways that are profitable and productive.

Mixed Model

In *Emotional Intelligence* (1995), Daniel Goleman describes 25 emotional characteristics and aspects that include teamwork, collaboration, among many other things (Salazar, 2017). This is a mixed model, because it talks about how emotional intelligence is influenced both by the emotions and personality. An individual's personality differences contribute to how they will respond to the various emotions they experience. Here is how this model is used practically.

Self-awareness

This first step to responding to any emotion is self-awareness, wherein a person recognizes the emotion in themselves, understands why they are feeling that way, and decide how they will respond. It requires acknowledging the emotion and writing it down or reflecting on it. Self-awareness is also related to self-confidence.

Self-regulation

After becoming self-aware, the person must decide what they will do with their emotions. They have to find ways to self-regulate and monitor their emotions, so they do not become out of control. This includes stress-relieving activities, such as exercise, meditation, prayer, taking a hot shower or bath, and aromatherapy. In addition, practicing mindfulness and positive self-talk are important ways that a person can self-regulate and live their lives free of emotional drama.

Motivation

In addition to our regulation of emotions, we must have a motivation for what we are doing. Having the right motivation is key to reaching our goals and will make us more successful in the long run.

Empathy and Social Skills

We need motivation and regulation of our emotions, but we also need a way to relate to other people. Empathy helps us to see from the perspective of others and strengthen relationships. We need to empathize with the emotions of others. It helps us to respect those around us.

The Trait Model

Petrides et al. (2009) discovered a model that looks at emotional intelligence through personality traits (Salazar, 2017). The trait model describes emotional intelligence in relation to a person's ability to understand his or her emotions. Traits of a person are based on an individual's self-awareness, but they cannot be measured objectively. This model looks at the different parts of a person's personality and then analyzes it in light of their emotional intelligence. Individuals can use this model to understand themselves more holistically.

As you can see, emotional intelligence can be described using a variety of models, which look at how it all works. Emotional intelligence is not easy to summarize in a few sentences or even paragraphs, because it is influenced by a lot of factors including family background, country, personality, gender, among many other variables. Having the knowledge of emotional intelligence is beneficial and helpful to everyone who learns more about it. It is vital that we find ways to understand and manage our complex emotions, so we can live happier and more meaningful lives.

Chapter 3:
Emotional Self-Regulation

Maybe you're considering emotional intelligence and you're not sure where to begin. You don't know how to boost your EQ, because you haven't figured out how it works. Perhaps, you are a thinker, who has creative ideas about how the world works, but you struggle to understand your emotions. You are not alone. There are definitely a lot of people who cannot comprehend their feelings. They simply do not know how to deal with them. So, they struggle to find ways to tackle different problems they might encounter. Let's look at some tips about where you can start in this journey to accept, comprehend, and deal with your own emotions.

Label your Emotion

One of the first steps to regulating our emotions is to label the emotions we are feeling. This includes making statements, such as "I'm feeling sad today, because _____." After identifying your emotion, you should explain why you feel that way. Try to find an objective reason for your emotion, because then you can understand your feelings at that time.

Become an Expert on Yourself

The second thing you can do to become more self-aware and regulate your emotions is to become an expert on your own profile. Study yourself. Get to know yourself. You should know who you are, your goals and objectives for life, as well as your relationships with others. It is also crucial that you learn what emotions that you experience regularly and what you can do to leverage positive emotions and deal with negative emotions. Track down your emotions by writing about them in a journal. You can look and see how you are feeling on different days and gauge how you have been able to overcome difficult times. When you journal your thoughts and feelings, you will become more self-aware and able to handle everyday challenges.

Another way to know yourself is by studying your personality. If you haven't already, take the Myers-Briggs personality indicator, which describes sixteen different types of people. You can analyze your personality and think about all the things that describe you. If you know more about your personality, then you will be able to understand yourself more clearly. When you understand your personality, you can also know how you interact with others and why you feel a certain way. Then, you might say to yourself, "That's who I get along with more" or "Aha! That's just how I feel!" When you study your personality more deeply, you will discover things about yourself that you didn't understand before.

You can also get to know yourself more by asking others their opinions about you. Ask them to comment on who you are and your unique personality. A close friend, mentor, or significant other could tell you a lot of things about you that you might not have been able to spot yourself. They can also tell you about blind spots in your life that you didn't know about before.

In our lives, we are the only ones who know ourselves the best. It is important for us to know who we are, what makes us tick, as well as what sets us off. For example, if you know that you get stressed on the road when you're running late for work, you should try to get out of bed earlier and leave at least 20 minutes beforehand, so you would feel more secure. Finding ways to regulate your emotions starts with a proactive mentality that will help you reach your objectives. Work on it. You can do it.

Don't Always Think that Emotions Need to be Fixed

It is important to realize that not all emotions are bad. In fact, every emotion is a valid response to a given stimulus. Our emotions are an important part of our humanity, and they indicate how we are feeling and how we should respond to a situation. What we need to do is figure out how we can respond appropriately to a situation. It is perfectly acceptable to have negative feelings. For example, we might be bothered by a person who is disturbing the peace outside and making noise. That might provoke us to go to the window in anger and shout at the person outside and raise our voice. Or, it could lead us to say to a person, "Shhh…please be quiet." With every negative emotion, there is a way to have a positive emotional response. Also, we might experience a negative emotion when we see a bear coming after us in a forest. This might activate our fight or flight response of fear. Then, we would flee the scene. It was a negative emotion, but it incited to us that we needed to take action and save our lives. Emotions can be self-defense mechanisms that we can use when we need them. Although an emotion may seem negative at the time, we can still exhibit valid feelings that need to be expressed.

Having said that, not every emotion tells the truth. We might be worried about a situation that we shouldn't worry about. For example, we might worry about missing a train or flight and stay up all night thinking about it. We might imagine worst case scenarios and be anxious about the future. The truth is, however, a lot of our worries never come to pass. They are simply figments of our imagination that have run wild. Many times, we need to rely more on our logic and rational thinking to make our decisions and not think about what could happen.

All things considered, we must see all emotions as valid responses to something and that they are not a problem to be fixed. Instead, they are something that we can continue to study and understand.

Train Your Mind to Recognize Emotions Based on Your Psychological Response

The fourth thing we should do is train our mind to recognize our emotions, based on our psychological response. Think about something that makes you angry. Maybe it is being stuck on Interstate 81 in traffic on your way to work. When you see the cars, buses, and semis bumper to bumper, you immediately feel your blood pressure rising and you want to escape the situation. You may also find yourself yelling (to yourself) at the other drivers of cars and buses on the road. As an emotionally intelligent person, you would recognize why you behaved this way, based on your prior psychological response to the feeling of anger.

Another example is if you are giving a presentation at a conference. You might recognize the sweaty palms, blood rushing to your face, or your heart rate rising as a symptom of nervousness about public speaking. Then, you would know what you would need to do to calm yourself down and train yourself to respond maturely to the situation. For example, you could tell yourself, "You're going to do awesome! You prepared for this. It's going to be amazing. You're going to blow them out of the water!" By pumping yourself up with positive self-talk, you will feel a lot more confident.

Case Study #1:

Devin was a very emotional man. Although he wasn't emotionally expressive in public settings, he would often repress his emotions. Devin would get depressed sometimes and he did not know why. He would suddenly feel slowed down and unable to operate at work. He would be slow in completing his tasks and unable to keep going. Also, he struggled with motivation to get things done. As a result, he would walk into work late after having slept little the night before. He was exhausted and in a lot of pain. Devin also had a bad drinking habit, which made him lose more sleep. Devin had low self-esteem, because he was not emotionally self-aware. Instead, he was repressing his emotions and self-medicating, but nothing was working.

Recognizing that he had a problem, Devin went to see a therapist, who helped him understand his feelings. His counselor told him, "Devin! I know that you are feeling down, but you should ask yourself why. Think about what was going on in your life before you were depressed. Write down your thoughts and feelings prior to that time. Think about what you can do to deal with that in the future. I think that becoming self-aware requires you to be reflective. I want you to start doing that next week and come back and tell me what you find out."

After this meeting, Devin started reflecting on his emotions. He thought about all the things he was doing every day. And then, he considered his own personality and how things would make him happy or upset him. Devin deeply contemplated his emotions, which helped him feel better about his life.

Upon completing this training, Devin understood that he could be the master of his emotions. No longer was he a slave to his emotions. He was in control of them. He didn't have to be overpowered by negative emotions. Instead, he could be proactive in dealing with them. Eventually, he could monitor when he was about to become depressed and catch himself before falling. It helped him manage his time, because then he wouldn't go off the deep end. At the end of the day, he was more productive at work and could motivate himself in whatever circumstances he was in. It was a success story.

Case Study #2

Jessica was frequently overcome by negative emotions. She was a mother of three boys, and she became upset with them all the time. When the boys would fight, she would scream at them to the point of losing her voice. Not to mention, Jessica was working three jobs to take care of her family. As a single mom, she had no one to help her around the house and she struggled to find daycare for her boys. She encountered a lot of stress that she was unable to express to others around her. It was overall very difficult. Many days, she thought that her world was about to collapse on her.

Realizing that she had a problem with anger management, she went to see a counselor who taught her mindfulness practices which would help her manage her emotions. She did some cognitive behavioral therapy (CBT) sessions and was able to calm herself down when she felt like she was going to fly off the rails and become enraged. Jessica learned how to identify her complex feelings and the emotions she was experiencing at a given time. She became more proactive in dealing with her feelings, so she would not get into negative territory repeatedly. Although she knew that her life was filled with stress and anxiety, she knew that she could control her emotional reactions and manage her emotions.

Soon, Jessica discovered how to regulate her emotions. She understood what stressors were causing her to act out and that she could control how she responded in those situations. Because she matured emotionally, she could help her sons live more fruitful and productive lives. She taught her sons manners and modeled good behavior. As children tend to watch their parents closely and their emotional reactions to situations, they learn a lot from watching their mother and father. The three sons watched their mother carefully, as she transformed into a calm and peaceful person. They realized that they needed to improve their behavior, so they worked on their conduct. It helped a lot. The boys became more obedient and respectful to their mother. Emotional regulation helped improve this situation.

Emotional self-regulation is an important part of emotional intelligence. It all begins with being more self-aware. We must become more aware of our emotions, so we can react appropriately to given situations. This often varies based on our gender, personality, unique characteristics, among other things. Before we can behave appropriately, we must recognize how we instinctively react to different situations and monitor what the best responses are. This will help us to regulate our emotions and be freer to express them in a positive and healthy way.

Chapter 4:
Self-Control of Negative Emotions

For us to learn how to manage our emotions, we must develop self-awareness that shows when things become too difficult for us to handle. We should write down our thoughts in a journal and put things down on paper that detail our emotional state. We should also understand how we respond to each situation. For example, if we become angry, we might throw a tantrum, start yelling or screaming, or we might be red in the face. Conversely, if we are sad or depressed, we might cry or become reclusive. Once you have recognized what your response is to each emotion, you can decide if it is the right way to respond. Consider how you could have reacted differently and changed the result of the situation.

Emotional regulation is something that we have to continually be mindful of as we practice it. It is something we must demonstrate to others, but it is not something you can simply tell another person how to do. Therefore, we need to show you how it can be practiced in everyday life through a lot of case studies that illustrate our points.

Anger

When we become angry, we tend to go off the edge into a tantrum or fit of rage. Anger is one of the fight or flight emotions, which causes us to react intensively and defensively. It is easy to blow a fuse if we are not mindful of how we are feeling. Furthermore, we must find ways to creatively and effectively manage this emotion. Let's look at a case study of a person and how he deals with his anger and consider what would have been a better way to react.

Case Study

Heath tended to always go into tantrums at work. He would get angry and curse his luck, especially when his computer would stop working. One day, his computer shut down in the middle of a task, which caused him to lose all his work for that day. He became red in the face and started shouting at the computer screen and made a scene in front of everyone. All his coworkers witnessed his anger and saw how dangerous his behavior became. When a person gets mad, they often can become a danger to those around them.

How Could Have Heath Behaved Differently?

Instead of blowing his fuse and creating a scene, Heath could have gone to the men's room and simply released his anger. Additionally, he could have gone on a long walk and tried to think out loud and get it out. Alternatively, he could have listened to his favorite upbeat and catchy songs, which would help distract him from the situation and put him in a happier place. Finally, he could have closed his eyes and practiced mindfulness by concentrating on the current moment and counting from one to ten. Then, he could be conscious of how he was breathing.

How He Could Have Used Mindfulness

One of the best ways that people can learn to manage their emotions is by practicing mindfulness. It helps people get on the right foot, because they can consider the present moment and their surroundings. They can easily lift their spirits out of a dark and depressing place. When they get ready to go off the edge, they can calm down their feelings that can easily disarm them and lead them to do regretful things. Heath could have used some meditation to soothe his troubled mind. Then, he wouldn't have flown off the handle and wanted to break a chair or throw something on his desk.

Anxiety

Isaac was a perfectionist in his work. He used to beat himself up whenever he made a mistake on the job. He had very high expectations of himself, because he had attended Brown University and graduated magna cum laude. As an ambitious and highly successful student, he had wanted to achieve his dreams in his life. Like with many other high achievers, he battled depression and anxiety, including the imposter syndrome. Dealing with his insecurities, he wasn't able to easily cope with stress and negative emotions.

Isaac's imposter syndrome continued even well into his career, while working as a successful legal assistant for a famous law firm in Washington. Isaac was an INTJ, and he was a detail-oriented person. Although he could look at the big picture, he was also very concerned with the fine details of life. Even with his careful and meticulous attitude, he could still make some small mistakes in his work that would rock his world.

Isaac was his own worst critic. When he made the slightest of errors, the negative voice in his head would beat him up. One Tuesday morning, he was completing a high volume of work and was not feeling so good. After working for a long period, he became exhausted and lost track of what he was doing and then ended up losing a whole data set on his screen. It simply disappeared from view. When we realized what had happened, he yelled, "Ahhhh! How did that happen? I cannot believe it! What the heck am I going to do now? I might be sacked from my job! Or, something worse could happen, like..." Mortified by what had happened, he went through a series of negative thoughts, which caused him to be fearful for his career and job. He felt paralyzed by the train of intrusive negative thoughts that had entered his brain. He tensed up and became worried. Having been upset by this situation, he went home and sulked and didn't eat or drink anything for days. He only drank water. He lost some weight from this incident. His sleep was also not restful every night.

Within a few days, he recognized that he could correct the mistake he had made, and that everything would be fine. These minor mistakes could be corrected, and the situation was going to be alright.

Was This an Appropriate Response?

Although Isaac was mad at himself, he didn't respond appropriately and worried unnecessarily over a small mistake. He allowed his intrusive negative thoughts to take over his life and went into a tornado of emotions, which made it difficult for him to function afterwards. Additionally, he had repressed his emotions so much that he imploded. Because he did not get his feelings out, he became depressed and couldn't eat or sleep as a result.

How Could He Have Reacted Differently?

Instead of blowing up, he would have started by recognizing his negative emotions and sought to understand his feelings. He could have answered the negative critic in his head by saying, "Isaac, it's okay, man. You made an error. It's human. Everybody does. It's going to be ok. It will be fixed. No one is going to yell at you for this mistake. Don't worry, bro!" By using some positive self-talk, we could have silenced the inner critic that was turning the situation into a crisis. Isaac should have tried to spot the intrusive negative thoughts that were taking control of the wheel and tried to escape. Then, he could have responded by encouraging himself with positive words. Also, he could have talked to a buddy about his problem.

The takeaway from this story is that you have to be aware of your emotions and manage them effectively. You must bring visibility to your emotions, share them with other people in your life, and address them. It is crucial to work on developing self-coping mechanisms that will help you deal with all the problems in your life, so you don't get caught off guard in the moment and react negatively in a situation.

Depression

George felt depressed frequently, especially when his grades came back to him. He suffered from depression and anxiety, as he felt like he always had to compete with his older sisters to get the best grades. It brought him into a low state. He also was autistic, which caused him to get below average grades. This made him feel depressed. Although he did his best at what he did, he still felt like he was no good at everything. On the other hand, there was one thing he was good at, writing poetry. He could write poems and use words that were so beautiful and free-flowing that he impressed people around him. Although he was not an eloquent writer, his poems spoke truth to the given situations in which he found himself. One of his buddies knew of his talent and wanted him to use it to the best of his ability. He tried to get him to submit his poems to a journal.

George went to a therapist, who told him he needed to be more positive and say encouraging words to himself. He told George, "You need to find ways of showing yourself grace and love and telling yourself that you are a good person. In fact, you are great. You're awesome. You're so talented, George. Maybe you don't get high grades, but you are talented in other ways that are just as important." George eventually understood this and he started to encourage himself. Whenever he received a bad grade, he told himself, "It's okay, George. You will do better next time. This is one bad grade, but you'll have another chance to do better. You can do it!" With the help of his two older sisters, he was able to raise his grades from Ds and Fs to Cs and Bs, which improved his morale and self-confidence. In the end, he was able to pass with flying colors. George felt satisfied with his life and was able to surmount the challenges of depression by self-affirmation and dedication to improvement in his school work.

Techniques that Work

When you're feeling sad, depressed, angry, anxious, or stressed, it helps to practice self-talk. You should examine your situation and see how you can bring out the positive. Try to push out the negative criticism in your mind and think about what you can do to counter the negative thought with a positive one. Close your eyes, count from one to ten, and focus on your breathing. Think about the current moment and don't allow yourself to go off the deep end. Rather, find ways you can take advantage of the current moment. Don't say things that are offensive to yourself. It will only make you feel worse. Calm down and sit and think about the things that you have been given in this life. Be thankful. Life is not meant to be a place where we worry about everything, but rather a place where you can thrive and use your gifts to achieve great things. Don't allow the hard moments to overcome you. All things are possible. Cheer up and keep rooting for yourself, so you can come out of the tunnel stronger than ever.

Negative emotions are a continual presence in our lives. They can easily overpower and disarm us at different moments. As we exercise our emotional intelligence, we can leverage the positive emotions and manage the negative ones that cause us trouble.

While we may feel that the negative always seems to beat the positive, when you have a positive mindset, then you will not have to listen to the intrusive negative thoughts that may be circling around like a cyclone in your head. Instead, you can silence that voice like you would your mobile device. You can be in control of your feelings and live a happier and more productive life. All things are possible; believe it.

Chapter 5: Experiencing Emotions as a Student in School

School days are some of the most enjoyable and stressful days of our lives. We are just developing as young people. Education is an important part of how we are molded and shaped. Emotional education is a valuable of our coming-of-age story, which helps us to know how to recognize the emotions within ourselves and understand how others feel, as well. Emotions in childhood can be particularly intense because of the various developmental factors and outside influences. The psychology of a student is sensitive to environment and can easily be affected by trauma, abandonment, neglect, among other negative things. Let's look at some case studies, which give examples of students and how they are influenced by emotions growing up.

Case Study #1:

Alexandra was a quiet child growing up. She was introverted and didn't want to be around other girls. Instead, she wanted to remain in her inner world, minding her own business. She would draw, sing, and dance, all by herself. As a student, she was quiet in class. She would not participate or raise her voice, because she was afraid of being judged by others. Additionally, she was not very confident. Whenever her teachers called on her, she would perk up and her heart rate would go off the charts. It was almost like she was about to have a panic attack. Then, a lump would appear in her throat. She could barely breathe. It was hard. Then, she muttered the right answer. The teacher said, "That's correct. Thank you, Alexandra." Immediately, she felt better and her heart rate returned to normal.

Case Study #2:

Samuel was always chasing the "A." He got a surge of energy whenever he would get As on his tests. He would feel so excited to receive it. It was like he was getting some kind of injection of adrenaline every time. Samuel was a conscientious student, who always did his homework faithfully and committed himself to his group projects. Once he got into college, his endless pursuit to get an "A" became an obsession. But suddenly, Samuel would be shocked when he got his first "B" on a test. Samuel became worried and started crying. He couldn't believe it. He thought he had studied hard enough for it. The subject was O-chem (Organic Chemistry), and he had done his best to cram as much as he could with his study group. It was a wake-up call for Samuel. He realized that he couldn't be the best at everything. He had to get "B's," although he had thought that "B" was bad and that "A" was acceptable. His experience in college changed his whole perspective on grades. To become more emotionally mature, Samuel started to accept the fact that he was going to get low grades occasionally and that it was ok. He could do better next time. It was a humbling experience for him but one where he needed to grow up and mature into an emotionally intelligent student.

Case Study #3:

Garrett was active as an athlete and a debate club member. He was so involved with his extracurricular activities that he became overwhelmed. He was not able to manage his time well. As a result, he was staying up late at night to study. Then, he would get poor sleep and arrive at school exhausted. With this continual pushing forward with his extracurricular activities, he started to feel burned out by it all. He became anxious and depressed and unable to cope under the weight of all the stress under which he felt buried. Garrett went to his guidance counselor to talk about what was going on. She told him to drop some things from his schedule that were getting in the way with his schoolwork. She told him, "Garrett, you're spending too much time on your sports teams. It's clearly causing your grades to slip. You need to be mindful of the scholarships that you want to get for your university. Don't lose sight of your goals. You can do it." Garrett listened to her words and got his act together. He stopped playing a few sports, because he had been on multiple teams. And then, he started going to tutoring to help him with the subjects that were giving him a hard time. He was able to bring up his grades from failing to passing within a few weeks. It helped him a lot.

Case Study #4:

Charlie was an introverted and selfish boy. He also didn't behave in class. He often talked to others and bothered them. In addition, he didn't listen to the teacher and would sometimes openly challenge him or her. Sometimes, he would simply not do his homework or assignments. He would sit through class or simply sleep, because he had not gotten a lot of sleep the night before and had numbed out playing "World of Warcraft" on his computer until 3am. Charlie's teachers realized he was going downhill and that his grades continually showed how he was doing. The problem was becoming serious, because Charlie's parents were not watching over him at home. He was left to be alone with his brother, Yannick, for whom he had to be the surrogate father, because no one was at home. His parents were always busy and did not take care of him or his brother. It was difficult for Charlie, because he carried a lot of resentment against his parents, who were not taking care of them. He hated them. And then, he took it out on them by misbehaving at school and not doing his work. It was difficult and yet, he was sad and depressed, because he was not getting the attention that needed to get at home. Thus, he became the bane of every teacher's existence. It was not easy. Yet, all the teachers had to become understanding of his situation and work with it as best as they could. Charlie was understandably frustrated and affected by the childhood trauma that had caused him to act out on his feelings and respond by being rebellious. In the end, he was troublesome and in a bad mood all the time. He would never look at the positive and instead would dwell on the negative. This would inevitably affect the other students around him. It had a bad influence on them. Pretty soon, all the students were complaining about him. It got so bad that Charlie had to leave the school. He only wanted to do what he wanted to do, so the school expelled him. In the end, he went to a special school for computer science, because that was what he was interested in.

What is Special about the Emotional Intelligence of Students

Students are at a moment of particular vulnerability in their lives. They are going through growth phases and are living in the same place as their parents. Until they reach college age, they are reliant on their parents for their emotional development. But as they go through their lives and experience different things in their lives, they become more exposed to different feelings. When they become adolescents, they start to experiment with things and rebel against their parents. But by the time they go to college, they reach an emotional maturity that keeps growing well into adulthood. Students are continually learning and growing in their emotional self-understanding. It takes a lot of time to mature. Once students reach a certain age, they can act on their feelings in more appropriate ways than before. They know how to regulate their emotions and can operate more effectively.

The Emotional Needs of Students

To meet the emotional needs of students, we need to focus on how we can educate them with emotional awareness, so they can deal with emotions in a culturally appropriate way. Students need to know how to manage their feelings, especially when they can get out of control. It is important to realize that students are in a vulnerable phase of their emotional development. As they encounter the stress of grades, peer pressure, among other things, they find themselves anxious, worried, insecure, among other feelings. Students develop their emotional intelligence over time. In the forthcoming chapters, we will talk about the growth and development of people from childhood to adulthood.

Chapter 6:
Experiencing Emotions
as a Teacher or Parent

When we think of emotional outbursts and other aspects of our lives, we often think of children and adolescents and their tendencies to act out on their feelings. However, we don't often consider what it is like to be a parent or teacher and how their emotional cycles play into how they live their lives. However, it is important to recognize the kinds of emotions that we encounter when there are parents and teachers, who are schooling their children in how to deal with their emotions. Parents and teachers likewise have emotions that need to be monitored and considered before we can think about the children. And we need to be sensitive to the emotional needs of each one, because then we can understand how to regulate our own emotions and how they can play into our lives.

Adults can become slaves to their emotions. This can happen in virtually every area of their lives. It is easy to become part of an emotional roller coaster that spirals out of control to the point where they can become drawn to outbursts and expressions of anger and frustration in front of others. And it is something that the children are watching, as they tend to mimic the behavior of the adults in their lives. When children see someone mocking another person who is disabled or struggling in their lives, they might also feel like they have a license to do the same thing. It is sad, but parents and teachers are the ones who make a lasting impact on the development of young children, and we have to see that they are the best models for children to follow. Otherwise, children will go down a dark path and see that they should be just like Mom and Dad or a teacher who is downright abusive toward students.

It is important to separate how each individual group of adults behave when using their emotions. Let's look at the role of parents and teachers and how they can be models for their children in emotional regulation, expression, and recognition.

Parents Model Their Emotions to Children

The first point to consider is how parents are being viewed by their children. Kids are watching their every move. Whenever a child views their parents, they see everything-- the good, the bad, and the ugly. Especially as a child grows up, the parents will demonstrate emotional regulation and self-control and they will have to follow suit with the upbringing of their parents, for better or for worse.

When a parent gets upset and throws a temper tantrum over something, then they demonstrate that it is right to do such a thing. When a child sees Daddy blow up about something on TV like the referees making a false call on a play in a football game, they feel that they need to also blow up whenever they get mad.

Emotional regulation is something that is taught first and foremost in the home. You can hear the calming demeanor of the mother in the situation as she says, "Frank, you have to not get so upset at the television. It's just not right. What will the children think?" The voice of reason always intercedes to help rescue the situation from a catastrophe. But, James and Justin are listening in on the conversation and hear what ensues from it. They pay attention to every detail of this exchange and know what it is that they want to do about it.

Parents should recognize their role as models for their children and do their best to control their emotions. But they should also show that their children should not repress their emotions. Instead, they should demonstrate the ways in which the children should express the emotions in a way that is constructive and less explosive than an emotional outburst. Parents need to see that their role is crucial to the emotional development of children and how they can interact more meaningfully with their peers and outside influences.

Because children are vulnerable and need constant support, they see how their parents deal with stress and anxiety. They watch as their mother struggles through work and finds time to do all the things she must do to watch the children, pay bills, do laundry, make food, wash the dishes, go grocery shopping--all the things that Mom does. They recognize that this is all stressing their mother out, so they go to lengths to deal with it and want to be on their best behavior to respect their mom. On the other hand, they may see Dad yell swear words at the TV, or curse people on the road when they get in his way, or watch as he throws a fit while punishing and whipping one of the children for disobeying. Children watch this and they see what it is like to be a parent, and how a parent deals with their emotions or their emotions them control them.

As a result of this careful observation of parents, it is crucial that moms and dads realize that they are truly the ones that their children look to for everything. Children are dependent on their parents for advice and other things. But there is also a level of trust that is given to parents, if they are good ones or not. Maybe their children will trust them, but maybe not. It is important, because children will not understand all of it, but they have to trust their parents to some degree. And if a child trusts his or her parents, then they can trust other adults in their life.

Building trust is a valuable part of the process of parenting. When you get the trust and support of your child, then you can make a friend for life. Your children will look to you for advice well down the line, which will help you a lot in the future years, when children must take care of you. And one part of that trust is guaranteeing that you can keep your cool. That is an important part of the process. If you can control your temper, then you show yourself to be a parent who is in control of all situations. On the other hand, if you frequently lose your temper, you demonstrate the lack of control that means that you cannot manage the situations in which you find yourself. It is vital to recognize this, because children look to their parents to be the ones who can help them and assist them in reaching their dreams. But if children cannot trust their parents, then there is a break in the relationship, making it hard to repair the damage that may come about as a result of bad parenting. What's more, you will have the lack of respect from your children for years to come, because you failed at giving them the proper education, which begins in the home. That is why trust-building is such a vital part of good parenting.

Case Study

Bill is a parent of three boys. He often would get into heated discussions with people and would sometimes blow his fuse at the drop of a hat. In addition, he was seen yelling insults to the TV over the false calls that were taking place at a college football match. He would even do this at the actual games, where he was surrounded by many people. Many people were noticing how he was doing this. Additionally, Bill would yell at his three boys and give them whippings for disobeying and tell them to go to their room. It was a never-ending cycle of Bill teaching his sons about how to emotionally express themselves. What he didn't realize was just how destructive this method was, and that it was causing his boys to be out of control even at school. His sons would get into trouble at school, because they got into fights with other young boys. The oldest son seemed to be doing fine, because he wanted to set a good example to the younger ones. But, the younger sons were getting into daily fist fights, and it was becoming a big problem. Part of the reason this was getting so out of hand was because Bill was behaving so badly in front of his sons. He was proving that he could not be in charge of his emotions. He gave his sons the license to lose their cool and to even become violent about it. Clearly, this was not right, but it was the kind of example he was setting for his sons, which obviously was not a good example to them. It was a problem that unfortunately would not be solved easily and would be an ongoing struggle for Bill and his family.

Teachers are Part of the School of Emotions for Students

Another part of the emotional education process is the teacher, who models emotional regulation for the students in the way that he or she behaves in the classroom. The teacher is the one, who like the parent, models to the students what good behavior looks like, as well as the consequences for good and bad behavior. The teacher essentially plays a role in schooling children in their education, which should have begun in the home. It is not something that is easy to do on their own. Teachers are never expected to take on the role of surrogate parents and try to school their children in a way that a parent should. Instead, they need to view themselves in the light of the role to which they have been entrusted and that is teacher. In this way, teachers must be careful to never overstep their authorities as teachers in disciplining the students. This is very important. But then, they must also not become so gentle and kind-hearted as to let the students do whatever they want. Instead, they must exercise discipline in such a way that leads to a controlled environment for children, where they can learn and play.

Teachers play an important role in getting the children to understand what proper behavior is and what the result of bad behavior is. They should demonstrate emotional restraint, never raising their voice or getting too angry at students but also never being too soft-spoken that they never want to scold their children. The thing is, teachers need to show that they can maintain control in a classroom, even if they are shy or introverted and unable to make their presence known in the classroom. But some of the best teachers can be the ones that just have to speak softly but powerfully to get the students' attention. Such teachers are able to captivate their students by their quiet nature but also realize that they have something to fear in that quality, which could easily become fearsome. There is some truth to the fact that the teacher should be both revered and loved at the same time, but not in a tyrannical way, such as in Machiavelli's *The Prince*.

As teachers model emotional restraint, they show how controlled they can be in the classroom. They demonstrate how it is important to not always express something that is bothering them. Sometimes, it is better not to speak at all when someone says something to you. Silence can be golden. Learning to hold your thoughts and not immediately respond is a sign of self-control. The teacher needs to demonstrate this to the student. Although students may become upset with the teacher for a grade given to them, the teacher needs to prove to the student that they are more mature and that they know how to handle such a situation. Teachers need to show that they can handle challenges with grace and care but also with great assiduity. They must prove how much more they know than the students, not just the subject matter that students are studying, but about life, and pepper their lessons with character-building lessons, which will motivate and engage the students in something that is outside of the students' subject that they are studying but something that is totally relevant to their lives.

By making character-building relevant to the students' lives, children recognize the value of excellence not just in education but in the way that students behave. And that includes emotional expression. Students should be taught that it is okay to be angry with someone and that should be expressed. But also, students should be instructed in the ways to not blow up and mess up a situation, where other children get hurt in the process. Students should be knowledgeable in the ways to handle their emotions and know the consequences of others getting hurt over emotional tantrums and other things. In addition, students should be educated in the ways that they should be sensitive to other students' emotions, because that is a very important part of the maturing process.

How Teachers Should Recognize Emotions Within Themselves

Teachers should recognize that it is okay to experience both emotions of frustration and elation and excitement. Often, teachers will experience waves of highs and lows. It is inevitably part of the process of growth and development. Some days, teachers will feel like they are at 100%, doing great, and making a difference. They may feel enthusiastic and excited to be there. But then, another minute or hour or day comes around, and they feel completely awful and depressed, because they shouted at the students for being out of control. It is normal to go through this series of emotions. It happens all the time. Teachers have good days and bad days. It's part of the typical cycle of things. But the thing is, they have to know how to control their emotions so they don't let the bad days suck up too much of their energy, and also allow themselves to control the energy that they have on good days, so they can be at their best. This is a crucial part of the maturing cycle of being a teacher.

As a teacher, you must recognize that you have these emotions. They are part of your makeup for a reason. Occasionally, you will feel the pangs of negative emotions, which seem like they are bringing you down. And sometimes, you will feel the surge of negativity that makes you want to have a shouting match with another student. Then, other days, you might be on cloud nine, wanting to shout from the rooftops to express your excitement as a result of a successful lesson. In any case, you must watch where you leap and you have to keep in check every emotion that you express, because the children are watching you. They watch your moves and how you behave. Therefore, you must be wary in the way that you act, because it can come back to bite you in the ways that the children behave in your class. In particular, if you set a bad example for the students, then they may feel like they have a license to do the same thing. It is a pattern-setting behavior.

In this way, like a parent, the teacher must be mindful of their own behavior and not set an example that is different from what they expect from the children. In the end, children are like chameleons. They adapt to different environments and mimic the authority figures that are put in place in their lives, for better or for worse. Furthermore, it is important to keep in mind how you act in the presence of children, whether you are a parent or a teacher, because children will understand better how to express their emotions.

Case Study

Tom was a fifth-grade mathematics teacher. He had received all the schooling to be a good teacher. He had gone to a prestigious education school to earn his M.Ed. in Mathematics Education. In addition, he had earned top grades at that school. Once he stepped into the classroom for the first time, however, he realized that it was a different ball park. He was surrounded by 30 chatty and exuberant fifth graders in a classroom. It was difficult for him to get used to it all. He became easily overwhelmed with all the names and faces and various needs of all the students. Frequently, he would come home with a mountain of work and cry his eyes out at the stress he was experiencing in class. The students were a bit rowdy and rambunctious. They were not easy to control, and over time, the lack of control and structure was taking its toll on Tom. One day, he completely lost it and yelled at the students and blew a fuse. It was a difficult moment for Tom. He realized that he had not been firm with the students before and had let it get out of hand over time. But then, he couldn't take it anymore, so he couldn't handle it. He told his co-teacher about what had happened. He felt ashamed and depressed afterwards having drained all of his energy reserves. It was unfortunate but it was how he was feeling.

What Could Tom Have Done?

It is evident that Tom could have controlled his temper during this time, but he also needed to learn the skill of classroom management, which reveals the consequences of following rules or not and allows students to understand the basic structure of the class. It is highly likely that Tom had not worked out his classroom management strategy, which made it difficult for him to control the group of rowdy fifth graders. It is something that every new teacher struggles with to some extent. However, it is something that teachers need to be educated about: how to control their emotions, express them in a healthy way, and maintain order and structure in a classroom. This is what Tom needed to develop. Granted, every new teacher's struggle is different, but it is important to know how teachers can handle themselves emotionally so they can prepare to be good leaders toward the children that have been entrusted to them.

Teachers and parents are both among the most powerful influences in a child's life growing up. They are responsible for educating students in emotional, academic, and personal matters. It is important that they learn to manage their own emotions, be mindful of the appropriate responses, and model that for children and adolescents. Young children pick up on the cues of how adults act. When adults act inappropriately, children and adolescents see that and feel that it is okay to act the same way. Therefore, it is crucial that we find ways to reveal the appropriate and inappropriate ways to react to a given situation, so our children know how they should respond to their emotions. Finally, teachers and parents should never underestimate the power of emotions and how they impact our lives. They should see them as opportunities to raise a generation of emotionally intelligent children, who can change the world for the better.

Chapter 7:
Emotions Experienced in Childhood

Our emotional cycles begin to affect us from an early age. We begin to recognize emotions even before we're able to fully function as a human being. And as the child's brain develops to be about ⅔ of its full size, then emotions become a part of his or her development (Cherry, 2019). When a child is a toddler, he or she will be prone to temper tantrums, which cause them to act out on their emotions. Children are very sensitive in the way they express their emotions. And they require the utmost care in helping them to get out their emotions (Cherry, 2019).

It is clear that children can be very selfish, as well. They only think of themselves and don't think of others. This is particularly the case of children who are in one-child families, who have only had themselves to look after during their childhood. But children need to be taught how to cooperate with other children and recognize the emotions of others, because that will help them to make friends, forge bonds with others, and have a better relationship with those around them.

Empathy

Emotional intelligence in children is something that needs to be taught from an early age. Children need to be taught how to interact with their peers and think about how their actions affect not only themselves but also those around them. For example, say a child takes away another child's toy, the parent should instruct the child to know how to think about that situation. They should think about how the other child might have felt about it. The parent could give a lesson to his child and say, "John, you took away the toy from Cynthia. She is crying and unhappy about that. How would it make you feel if she took away your toy?" John replied: "I would cry too. It would not make me happy." Parents need to teach their children how to empathize with others and look after the emotional needs of those around them. Children can be unaware of what others around them are thinking or feeling, and this is very damaging to them. No wonder we have more fights in school or temper tantrums in the classroom or at home.

Emotional Regulation

Children also need to be taught how to regulate their emotions and practice mindfulness to calm down in the case of a temper tantrum, which can happen at any given moment. For example, say a child has a difficult time and wants to express their emotions but is getting angry and frustrated about it, they need to figure out how they can get out the negativity within them, but they don't know how to get it out of them. So, they explode and break something or yell and scream. This warrants emotional regulation in which a child can effectively calm himself or herself down and not respond negatively to a given situation.

One thing that could help children regulate their emotions is hitting a "pause" button, which enables them to effectively stop themselves from flying off the handle and causing stress to someone else. If they can effectively say, "NO!" to a loss of self-control, then they can move forward with their lives and be in control of their emotions. Giving children the chance to hit the pause button and count to ten and close their eyes will allow them to be more mature and able to handle all situations effectively.

Another thing that children can do to help with their emotions is to find ways to externalize their feelings by playing a musical instrument, doing some exercise, or writing in a journal. If your child is healthy, they will be better at regulating their emotions. It is vital to find ways to get your child to be mindful of how they are feeling at a given time, so they can contribute peacefully to their environment.

Teach Children How to Be Aware of Their Emotions

Children should also be instructed in how they can be more aware of their emotions as they develop, because they need to know about what they feel. Ask your child how he or she feels, because that will make a difference in how they can express their emotions. They need to get it out, especially when they are confused or upset and unable to understand what they are feeling.

Model Behaviors and Attitudes that Children Can Express

Adults are the models that children must follow, so they need to show good behavior that is friendly and well-regarded. If they don't exhibit this kind of behavior, then they will likely have no manners and be bad examples to others. Then, they won't function well in society. You want your child to behave well in public, so show them how you should say "please" and "thank you," and express manners in public. Children follow the examples of their parents and other adults around them.

Case Study: Daniel

Daniel was a child who had a lot of emotional problems that caused him to go over the edge frequently. He was a child who went to a private school in Korea. He was in the fifth grade. He often felt left out and didn't seem to fit in with his class. Many of the other students made fun of him and didn't make him feel welcome. They would insult him behind the teacher's back. Because the teacher could not speak Korean, it was hard for him to intervene into the various situations that caused the child to act up. Before this teacher had started working with Daniel, there had been a lot of problems that had to be addressed. Daniel had a difficult relationship with his previous teacher, which caused him to have even more hard feelings. Furthermore, he didn't like his brother and would hit him all the time. He never seemed to get along with anyone.

Daniel's teacher recognized that he was going through a hard time and wanted to help him as much as he could. He prayed for Daniel that he would grow up and mature and also gain emotional intelligence. It was not easy, but things got better. Daniel would have a lot of emotional tantrums. He would break pencils, stomp his foot, and run out of the room and cry. He didn't know how to control his emotions. It was very difficult for him to function, as a result. Many of Daniel's other teachers tried working with him. It was very difficult for everyone involved. Daniel's mother was also in low spirits, because she had tried everything. She didn't know what to do about it. She also wanted a miracle and for her child to change. Daniel had promised his mother that he would change.

The teacher started working with Daniel. He focused his attention on accommodating Daniel and giving him the things that he needed to do. He helped him with homework, constantly monitored his progress, and showed that he genuinely cared about Daniel. Daniel began to respect his teacher as well as others around him. He learned how to control his emotions. It was a great learning experience for him. Whenever he saw that he was going off the wall, he knew how to check himself and get back on the right track. It was a success story. In the end, Daniel did a lot better in school and was able to do all the things that he set out to do, because his teacher believed in him.

What We Can Learn from Daniel's Case

What we can learn from this case study is the power of patience and dedication to a child. Daniel's teacher recognized that Daniel was special and that he needed more care, and he showed him how he could behave and get his feelings under control. It was a great experience, as his teacher showed him love and affection that Daniel needed in his life. Unfortunately, it was difficult as he had not developed his own emotional intelligence. But after a while, he was able to do that. He knew how to recognize his own emotions and how they impacted others. Additionally, he was able to know how to regulate his emotions. This led to his overall success at school.

Childhood is an important phase for a child to develop emotionally. Children need to have the support and help of their teachers and parents, who can be the models to them for the kinds of behavior that can help them function in their lives. Without it, then they won't be able to regulate their emotions. They also won't be mindful of the emotions of other people around them. Consequently, they may feel that they don't know how to feel better when they get down. Teaching emotional intelligence is one of the most important things to impart to a young child, because they need to be aware of their own emotions, how they impact others, and how to put themselves in the shoes of other children and adults around them. It is crucial for children to know the proper boundaries in their lives and how they can become emotionally mature by the time they reach adulthood. Step by step, they can reach the level of a grown-up man or woman.

Chapter 8: Emotions Experienced in Adolescence

As anyone can tell, one of the most challenging periods of our lives is adolescence, because it is when our brains have not yet fully developed and we go through the phases of puberty, which is the process of becoming a man or woman. Undoubtedly, adolescence is a time in which teenagers are prone to fits of rage, wild behavior, and overall acting out on their feelings, which can lead to reckless behavior that is often unhealthy and can endanger other people around them.

Why is Adolescence So Tough?

Adolescence is a difficult period for emotional intelligence, because teenagers are not yet adults. They are still children in many respects. They still have feelings and emotions that they have had since childhood, but they are sensitive during their teenage years. Children develop their sexual organs, change their voice, experience the development of growth hormones, and undergo a lot of other bodily processes which contribute to their overall sensitive emotional state. Because they are going through so many changes, they are prone to being very emotional and unable to control themselves. At times, they might engage in risky and rebellious behavior, because they cannot control their emotions.

With adolescence, there is the influence of movies, television, music, and peers, of course. Teenagers are swayed by the way their friends are, and they mold themselves to think and act like others, as well. When they see their peers act a certain way, they want to act that way, too. They are a conformist group in many respects. Individualism is not as valued, so much as a person's ability to give in to peer pressure, which is what teenagers do all the time, for better or worse.

Building an Identity

In addition to peer pressure, teenagers are working on building their identity, while they are growing up. They have not completely formulated in their heads who they are. Instead, they are focusing on what everyone around them is doing and conforming. Often, teenagers don't want to be individualistic during this stage out of fear of what their peers might think of them, so many times, in many cultures, they will simply not act out of the norm of what is expected of them. Adolescents don't like to be told what to do, however. In these cases, they can become very rebellious and want to disobey their parents or authorities, because they act out on their feelings.

Rebellion Against Authority

Teenagers question the authority of their parents and teachers. They test the grounds on different levels. They can become quite moody and disobedient when they don't get their way and often, they are disrespectful toward adults, especially those who are not using their authority in a wise manner. Teenagers are quick to judge and realize when authority figures are doing a good job or not. They see through the sinful patterns of adults in their lives and know when adults are doing bad things. Therefore, they will not trust adults, who are not modeling decent behavior and they will criticize them and not want to obey them. Because teenagers are moody and disrespectful, they will show their emotions in violent temper tantrums with their parents. In many cases, counselors and therapists must intervene when there are struggles between parents and teenagers, because the situation can escalate to an emergency.

Sensitivity of Teenagers

In addition to their rebellion against authority, teenagers can be sensitive to different situations in their lives, including difficult home lives. They find themselves becoming more emotional and reactive to different circumstances, because they don't know how to handle their own emotions. With their hormones working overtime, hair growing in their pubic areas, voice changing, among other life changes, many teenagers struggle with these things. They don't fully understand what is going on and feel vulnerable to the things that are going on in their lives. They can be distracted from school, engage in risky and reckless behavior, and get into legal trouble, as well. It is important to bear in mind how sensitive teenagers can be.

Case Study

Mr. Henry was a teacher at a private school in South Korea. He taught secondary students in his class who were very engaged in his lessons, but they had a lot of relationship struggles. Mr. Henry did not speak Korean, so he was not able to engage in interpersonal conflicts that would inevitably arise between different teens in his class. The students would be moody and argue with one another. They would insult each other, but he was not aware of what they were saying. It was a difficult moment for his communication with the students. Additionally, sometimes, the students would not be motivated to do things because they were so tired. Understanding the emotional needs of his students, Mr. Henry tried giving students more opportunities to do their assignments in class. He respected their need for rest at night. And he tried to be sensitive to the relational needs of the students, knowing that acceptance by peers is something that many students struggle with in high school. He tried to pair up students who felt left out, and in the end, he was able to experience more harmony in the classroom.

Important Considerations When Dealing with Teenagers' Emotions

When you are dealing with teenagers, whether you are a parent, school counselor, teacher, mentor, or other adult in their lives, you need to recognize what needs to be done during this phase of life. It is important that you are sensitive to the needs of teens. They may need to have someone to listen to them whenever they may be flying off the deep end. Because teens may experience intense emotions, they may not know how to handle them at a given time. You should be understanding of this. Know that it is in some cases a symptom of their experience that they would be so emotional. Teens are still understanding who they are when they are growing up. They don't know themselves fully yet. They are still figuring out their personality, likes and dislikes, and things they are passionate about. Sometimes, these are thrust upon them by their parents and other influences. But in the most ideal cases, teens are left to figure out what makes them passionate.

Providing Help for Mental Health

One of the crises in teens today is mental health. Many teens commit suicide each year due to depression or other serious disorders. Getting help for mental health has never been more important. Depressive disorders can develop when a person is a teenager, as this is an emotionally tumultuous time. When you provide support to your teen, they will greatly appreciate it, and you could save a life. Mental health is a hard thing for many people, including teenagers who are still developing. It is crucial to find ways of getting the medical and therapeutic help for teenagers. Go see a doctor or counselor for more information. Don't hesitate to seek help, because it can save lives. Providing support is one of the biggest ways we can effect change in the lives of teens around us.

One way that people are doing this is by providing mental health days to students. In Oregon, teens have persuaded the government to provide five mental health days every three months (BBC). It is a great initiative that will help more students seek help when they need it. About 17% of eighth graders have contemplated killing themselves (BBC). So, it is crucial to give students a space where they can seek to receive treatment for their mental health conditions. Many students are struggling with anxiety and depression. By giving students the chance to rest from school or take time off, it will encourage them to go to the doctor, get therapy or medication, and live a more balanced and stress-free life. This will help transform the lives of millions of teens, who don't know how to deal with depression or other mental illnesses.

In addition to this initiative, there are more advocates who are marketing Mental Health Awareness Month, which encourages support to fight the stigma of mental illness. It will make it easier to get people advocating for those in need. It is crucial to do things like this to encourage teens to get the help and support they need to grow up and mature into emotionally healthy adults, who will lead the world.

Case Study

Jericho was a teen who struggled a lot his senior year of high school. When he was 17 years old, he was diagnosed with manic depression. He had a manic episode where he imagined that he was going to take a helicopter to France. He stayed up all night and wrote a letter to the Consulate of France to send him there. The next morning, he arrived at school completely delusional and spaced out. He was feeling exhausted from everything, although Jericho was a very put-together teen who had succeeded in school. He got straight As and was invested in his education. However, his mental health was not in good condition. He had no friends or support group, which made his battle with mental illness that much more difficult.

After his first episode, Jericho had to spend some time in the psychiatric ward of a hospital. He was with other teens, many of whom were suicidal and had self-harmed. He felt very out of place at that time. He became depressed even with the medication that he was being given there. Soon, he was able to return to school. Jericho got the support he needed. His classmates were helpful and wanted to talk to him, although he was introverted and shy. His teachers were kind and understanding and wanted to give him extensions on his assignments. Jericho had to go through the entire year with ups and downs. But with his experience, he learned how to train his emotions and not fly off the handle. Through a combination of therapy and medication, he was able to control himself whenever he felt that he was going off the wall. In addition, he learned how to cope with his negative feelings by praying to God and meditating through mindfulness exercises. In the end, Jericho discovered ways to know himself and how to manage the symptoms of his mental illness. It helped a lot. This was a success story.

It is vital to realize that teenagers are at a developmental cycle of their emotions. The human brain does not completely mature until a person reaches age 25 for men and 21 for women, so they will constantly be growing until early adulthood (Brodwin and Gould, 2017). We must recognize that teenagers are also in a vulnerable stage of emotional development. They need continual support and guidance to navigate the waters of adolescence, which is a scary, confusing, and difficult moment of their lives, where they are beginning to understand who they are and what interests them. Therefore, empathy and encouragement from adults will help them develop into responsible, caring, and emotionally intelligent adults.

Chapter 9: Emotions in Adulthood at the Workplace

After having gone through childhood and adolescence, we enter into adulthood having formed our emotional core. We know who we are and what we are capable of doing. As we go into adulthood, we understand how we can deal with our various emotions. We have a mature way of coping whenever we have negative emotions. We have developed a variety of techniques that help us to go through our lives. But then, there are still adults figuring out their emotions and how they work. It is not an automatic process, but it is something that can be mastered over time after training and experience. Emotional maturity comes from the ability to recognize your emotions, affirm them, and respond in appropriate ways that will help and encourage others.

How to Develop Emotional Maturity

As you become an adult, there is a lot more stress in life. You have more responsibilities at work and at home with the family. As you go through this phase, you will notice how you become more worried and prone to becoming depressed under the weight of all the pressures in your life. This comes with the territory. Many times, we must have a lot of difficulties that come into our life, because it tests our ability to be resilient and steadfast. Developing emotional maturity often requires us to be tested by fire, because then we can be refined by the trials and tribulations we may have in our lives. Life is not meant to be easy. Often, it requires a lot of hard work and dedication. That involves blood, sweat, and tears. We have to go through the difficulties in this life with joy and patience. Then, we can develop our maturity personally and emotionally.

To mature emotionally is a process that can be lifelong, but it is something that can happen at any stage. Adults are expected to have their emotions in line, because they are to set the example for their children and other young people in their lives. They must learn to be self-controlled, although much of society still makes people remain in the pubescent teenage-angst mode, because people don't want to take responsibility for their actions and behavior and end up remaining immature and unwilling to move forward. This mentality also exists in different people. What is important is a willingness to grow and mature. That is something that is within a person. Then, they can move on to bigger and better things.

The Stressors of Everyday Life

For adults, there is so much to be stressed about - bills to pay, people to please, assignments to be completed, places to go, mouths to feed...the list goes on. There are many things that are difficult about life and they don't make adulting an easy task. Yet, many people have to grow up and do the things they don't want to do. It is not simple and requires a lot of growth and a steep learning curve. But once you get used to it, then you feel like anything is possible. You can do all the things you set your mind to. You don't have to let the stressors of everyday life get in the way. You know that you can easily overcome the situations in which you find yourself. You will have developed a lot of resilience and time-tested faithfulness. That is not an easy thing to get to, but after a while, you can face the day and deal with all the problems that may come your way.

Why Many Adults Struggle to Keep It Together

Amid all the emotional maturity, many adults still struggle to keep it together, because their emotions are not in order. They still have the adolescent fears and emotional temper tantrums that they threw when they were a teenager. Many adults still remain immature, and they spend more than they make, getting themselves into financial trouble, just because they wanted to get that next big-ticket purchase on credit. As a result, many adults are struggling to live a life full of meaning and enjoyment. Instead, they are swimming through the slogs of despair, anxiety, and immaturity, which are keeping them from achieving their dreams. A society makes them go into debt for education and other things, because it is positively encouraged, but it makes millions of people have a profile of manchild or womanchild. It is sad but true. Too many people are not taking responsibility for their lives, much less their emotional maturity. Therefore, there is no better time than now to explore the topic of how to have a better emotional life to be a positive influence on the next generation.

Emotional Intelligence at Work

Adults have to remain emotionally mature, because they have to relate to those around them. They can form meaningful relationships with people at work, empathize with those in need, and enhance their social life. There are different ways that you can improve your emotional intelligence at work, so you can have a productive and fruitful career. Everyone wants to be successful. Look at the following tips that will help you become more in tune with your emotions and able to tackle all of life's demands.

Working Alongside Others

One way that emotional intelligence helps you is by giving you the chance to interact with people who are different from you. Not everyone thinks, looks, acts, or feels exactly the same way you do. Everyone is unique in their own way. It is important to respect the individual differences of other people. You should also seek to find common ground with the people in your life. When you learn how to work with other people, you learn how they feel and think. You understand their differences and how those can bring new insights to the table. You begin to appreciate different perspectives, which enhances the dialogue that you may have in the workplace. Therefore, if you have a higher emotional intelligence, you will be able to work alongside a lot of people, who have different communication styles, interests, and passions from your own. And that is great. Not everyone needs to look exactly the same you. Perhaps, you want to find people who listen to the same music as you or watch the same movies as you do. Granted, everyone in this world looks for commonalities.

What's more important is when two people who are different can come together and communicate effectively. That breaks down barriers and allows you to come to an agreement about different things. It's diplomacy in action.

Strengthening Social Skills

When you have an ability to work with a variety of people, you may also find yourself hanging out more with the people in your workplace. You will be more of a social butterfly, who people want to be around. When you can gauge how people feel, you will be able to socialize more efficiently and you will have more friends, as a result. Emotional intelligence allows you to relate to other people's feelings, so you can have deep and meaningful relationships with them. You will seek to have strong bonds with others, which will help you form lifelong relationships with others. Often, people with higher EQ can reach other people in ways that people with high IQs cannot. Think about it. You may be able to understand other people on an intellectual level, but you might not have a sense of humor. Then, you might not be able to connect with others, because you're so focused on the thinking component but not enough on the relational level. That is why strengthening your EQ by having a good sense of humor and connecting with people can help you bring joy to their lives and helps you make friends more easily.

Be the Positive Hero in Others' Lives

Another thing that we have to do is be a positive influence in others' lives. Try to look on the bright side of everything. Many people in our lives might be a Negative Nancy or Ned, and that unfortunately brings many people down and causes them to become negative and pessimistic. Instead of following suit with them, you can find ways to encourage or brighten someone else's day. Compliment someone. Say to them, "You look great today! You're going to do an amazing job!" or "Keep doing it. You're doing great work!" Be a positive and encouraging presence in the lives of others, and you will see that your social EQ will improve. It will help you feel better about your life. Plus, you can encourage others to be positive with you. Infusing the room with positivity will make everyone feel great. Then, you will find that people want to spend more time with you. They will love your infectious attitude, as you smile and make them laugh. Becoming a positive hero means looking on the bright side, making a transformative influence on the next generation, and being the person on the sidelines cheering people on. It is a powerful force to be reckoned with.

Empathize with Others

Another important thing that we develop as adults is an ability to empathize with the feelings of others. It is something that should have been taught in school or in other places, but often it gets shoved aside. When we can empathize with the emotions of others, then we can see from their perspective. We feel what they are feeling, because we have been through something that is similar. Then, we can help support and sustain those around us who are having a hard time. When you see someone who is struggling under the weight of work, you can help a person by lending a hand at a small task that needs to be done. Or, you can be a listening ear to someone who needs to talk with you about what's going on in their lives. It is important to find ways to empathize with others, because then you can see a person and their humanity. You can help them out and be a supportive presence in their lives. We all need this from time to time.

Case Study #1:

Ken was a person who wanted to make a positive difference at the startup where he was working. There was a lot of negativity going on in the office. People were gossiping, complaining, and doing other things. At the beginning of his time there, Ken was bothered by this. He felt disturbed that people were being so negative. While Ken could have broken down and started complaining about it, he started to interact with the people around him. He started to develop his social skills and reach out to the people around him. He became a positive hero in his workplace. He would compliment different people in the company. Pretty soon, other people started following suit. They realized that he was making a positive difference and wanted to change their attitudes, so more people started being kind to one another. Other workers started to exchange kind words with each other. No longer were people griping or competing with one another. It became a great change for the company. Not to mention, people became more productive. They focused more on getting things done and less time on thinking about what was going wrong in the company. It helped. And later, the stock portfolio of the company grew and its online presence became more successful. Things were looking up for Ken's company, and it all started with his being positive and making other feel his happiness. In the end, the company grew from it and became successful.

Case Study #2

Nelson was one of the Negative Neds of his company. Every day, he brought down people in his company. He would complain about this and that. He talked about how much he hated the coffee that was in the office kitchen. He said that it was absolutely awful and that he wanted them to get better coffee. Not only that, but Nelson complained about his colleagues and would spread rumors about them behind their backs. People at the company were noticing how negative he had become at the office, and they were taking note. They didn't really want to be around him anymore. Nelson had low social skills, so he would alienate the people in the office. He was also an intensely selfish person, who would spread out his stuff everywhere. Sometimes, he would leave his belongings in the office kitchen without thinking of others. Nelson soon became depressed and didn't understand what he was doing wrong. He would have emotional outbursts at home, because he couldn't contain his frustration. His wife tried to help him be positive, but it was not working. Nelson realized he had to get some help for his negativity. He needed to get some clinical assistance, so he went to see a therapist. His therapist told him to do some cognitive behavior therapy (CBT) to help with his anxiety and frustration. Moreover, he went to weekly therapy sessions. Through these sessions, he learned how to be more positive, focus on the given moment, and pause and think about how he was breathing and acting. Soon, Nelson became more reflective of how we was acting. He recognized when he was about to fly off the handle, and he could easily stop himself from going too far.

After six weeks of CBT, Nelson stopped having fits of rage. He also stopped complaining at the office. He became a more welcoming presence at work. He also started to engage in conversations with his coworkers. He invited a few of them to coffee once. Before, he had always gone to the cafe by himself and didn't want to engage in conversations with others, because he had always repelled the people around him. Once the others had seen the powerful transformation in Nelson's life, they wanted to be around him. Nelson started to become interested in others, and he wanted to work for the welfare of other people. It was amazing to see how he became a social butterfly within two months. It was a fantastic result of therapy, hard work, and a desire to be more positive. In the end, everyone saw the difference it made. It made an impact on the workplace, thanks to the emotional intelligence of a transformed man.

To conclude, the emotions we develop in our adulthood impact those around us. They influence our children, spouses, coworkers, and other people in our lives. When we have more emotional intelligence, we have the power to be a changer in our communities. There is power in being a positive person in others' lives. When we can be positive and get to know people on an emotional level, we develop a stronger sense of connection, which creates ties that bind us together. As we grow and mature, we recognize how important it is to make connections with others. Once we have reached the adult stage, we know how to form relationships with others, so we can be productive and active individuals, who are shaping and transforming the world around us.

Chapter 10: How to Manage Emotions in Your Career

Throughout our career, we encounter a lot of emotions that are related to the work we do, because we have a variety of experiences that cater to our emotions. How do we deal with them? What do we do with these emotions? In this chapter, you will learn about how to manage negative and positive emotions in the workplace.

Emotions in the Workplace

Within the workplace, there is a lot of competition for the best jobs, assignments, among other things. You may not realize it, but in your workplace, many of your colleagues are competing against each other. That is because oftentimes this competitive spirit is not voiced. Instead, it is implied and can be seen in different people at different times. We must be watchful to avoid this kind of spirit. It only makes for miserable people. As you go about your life in your career, you will notice a pattern of negative emotions, which can impact you and your colleagues. Let's look at some examples.

Envy and Jealousy

Think about how you would feel if your friend got a promotion for doing the same work that you did. Although you did not receive public praise for the job you did, which turned out to be identical to that of your friend, you feel resentful and jealous of that person, because he got all the public accolades. But what did you get from it? Nothing. And you definitely don't feel good about it. Envy and jealousy are common emotions that you might experience in the workplace. They can destroy trust among individuals and make them turn on each other. In addition, they can cause you to have a negative relationship with others that will create a cut-throat environment. Competition can be a positive in some places, but often, it causes division and makes people jealous of others, who get a promotion of status.

How to Deal with Feelings of Jealousy

It is natural to feel jealous of others, who do better than we do, whether that is financially, professionally, or otherwise. We want what other people have and it causes us to be unsatisfied with the things we have. Unfortunately, this is a common problem to the human condition. But one of the things that we can do for ourselves is be thankful for all the things we have been given. Often, we are doing a lot better than we think we are. We are in good health, we have a decent salary, and we seem to be doing a good job for the company. Be thankful for those things. It is important to see the good in our lives and not only look at the things we lack, because then we can feel better about ourselves. There are a lot of other people in this world, who are struggling and don't have a good living situation. We should be thankful that we have not been put in desperate situations, where we have to beg for food or other things. When we look at our situations through that lens, then we will feel more satisfied with our lives. We will also stop comparing ourselves to other people, which is something that social media continually pressures us to do. When you have stopped comparing your life to other people, then you will feel a lot better about your life and happier, as well.

Case Study

Allen was working at a start-up company. He was a new employee, who had no experience beforehand. He was simply getting started. But he had a habit of always comparing himself to all the other employees. Allen was struggling to get some of his assignments done, but then he saw how his colleague Colleen was getting all her assignments done well and in little time. It made him jealous of her, and he resented the fact that she was doing well. Then again, Colleen had been in the company for 1.5 years; whereas, Allen had been there for only three months. Allen got depressed, because he was not doing well and feared that he might not get to stay at the start-up company. Then, one of his colleagues named Eric decided to mentor Allen and offer him advice. Eric told him, "Allen, you need to stop comparing yourself to other people. It is only discouraging you and making you miserable at work. Instead, focus on YOU and not anyone clse. Don't worry about what someone else is doing. Mind your own business. That is the most important thing you can do. You have to be mindful of all the things that you need to do, not what your neighbor is doing." Allen realized that he was doing this all wrong. He was ashamed of himself, but then he started doing what Eric told him to do. He stopped comparing himself to other people and got the work done he needed to complete. In the end, his performance greatly improved, because he no longer needed to look at what other people were doing. Instead, he focused on himself and what he could do to get better at his job. Allen became successful, and within six months, he got promoted.

Frustration with the Workplace

Another common emotion that we see in the workplace is frustration with working conditions, supervisors, and colleagues. It is something that we have to learn how to deal with, because there are always people we don't like to work with and things we don't enjoy about our workplace. It's not always easy, but to show emotional maturity, we need to do things to make things more uplifting and less frustrating. Of course, one way to evade the frustration is simply to quit your job and move on to another. But not everyone has that luxury. Sometimes, we simply have to stay at the same job and contend with the issues faced by employees at the company. Here are some common complaints that we might have.

Supervisors

Love them or hate them, we have to deal with supervisors in our workplace. Sometimes, they leave us to do our own thing and get things done independently. At other times, they micromanage us and leave us feeling frustrated and irate because they can't leave us alone to do the things we need to get done. Additionally, we may come into personal conflict with them, which can leave us feeling more angry and resentful toward them. But we must learn how to deal with them. Even if we don't like them, we still must work with them. That's not an easy thing, but it is necessary.

Colleagues

Some colleagues are downright frustrating to work with. They are annoying and cause a lot of trouble. In addition, they might gossip about you behind your back, which betrays trust and makes it harder for you to function in the workplace. Dealing with relational trouble with colleagues is one of the things that makes many people want to leave their jobs for something else. But for those who must stay at their job, they have to also find ways to contend with the situation.

Difficult Working Environment

Another turnoff for workplaces is the actual environment. Whether it is too hot, cold, stuffy, disorganized, or crowded, there are always a lot of things that people will complain about with the workspace. This is something that everyone needs to get used to and work with, even though it can cause people to feel frustrated. Not to mention that copier that is temperamental and will stop working in the middle of a print job. That makes everyone's lives miserable.

What to Do About Difficult Working Conditions

What should we do about difficult working conditions, whether that is with colleagues, supervisors, or a workspace environment? First, we need to seek to build harmony in our relationships. That is not an easy thing, but it is important to be obedient to our supervisors and have a meaningful relationship with colleagues. There will always be people we don't like to be around, but that doesn't mean we have to be a total jerk toward them. Instead, we can live peaceably with everyone. It is a principle that we need to follow all the time, how we can coexist with others around us. About working conditions, we should try to work with the various things we are given. Otherwise, we can invest in our own items. For example, if the office stapler is broken, we can simply buy our own office supplies. Don't seek to rely on the items in the office provided by the company. Take responsibility to care for your own needs and do so in order to not be reliant on anyone. That will help with your overall emotional state and enable you to be an independent and reliable professional.

Case Study

Rachel was a hardworking professional who wanted to get things done to a high standard. Yet, she, along with other colleagues at her workplace, was frustrated with the operations of the company. There were a lot of dysfunctional things happening. The management was sparse and unreliable. People were always MIA (missing in action), which made everything difficult and unpredictable. As a result, everyone had to pick up the slack for the missing management. It made everyone's lives miserable and more stressful. Rachel got very frustrated with it, but then she realized that she could handle it if she stopped complaining. Instead of becoming more irate about it, Rachel started to take the lead in her company. She took on more responsibilities at work and did so without making a fuss about anything. Then, she also tried to build relationships with others, including the management. She spent her lunches socializing with colleagues. Eventually, Rachel received a promotion for her hard work. She became a manager over the company. People saw her leadership potential, so she was rewarded for her hard work. Rachel did not expect that to happen. She was just trying to be the best employee she could be. However, she was able to become an impactful worker in her company, which led her to take on leadership at a place that really needed it. This was success with emotional intelligence at work.

Anxiety

Anxiety affects all different aspects of operations in a company. That includes finances, work-related performance, among other things. Think about when you have an evaluation of your performance at work. And suddenly, you have to prove yourself to your supervisor. It may make you anxious or worried about what you have done. You might have to put together a portfolio or other things that show what you have completed this quarter at the company. You must also compile a list of accomplishments you have made to contribute to the company. All of this can contribute to a great deal of stress in your life because it may make a difference in a company's decision to promote you, renew your contract, or other things.

We all have to deal with some anxiety in our lives. It is inevitable. It is not easy to be anxious at work, but sometimes we have to deal with it. We must be extra prepared for observations, evaluations, and many other performance-based assessments of our work. Instead of dreading these times, we must find ways to appreciate them. Take time to recognize that they are not meant to scare us or cause us to be nervous. Instead, they are opportunities for us to showcase our talent and skill to our supervisors. Therefore, we should use them to our advantage and not feel as if our employer is seeking ways to test us or make us feel uncomfortable in the performance evaluation process. Think of the opportunity to receive a raise afterward. That is often enough of a motivation to get us to do our best job on the evaluation.

Case Study

Alexander was a teacher at a private school in Washington, DC. He taught English as a Second Language (ESL) to high school students. He had a hard time his first year at the school with a lot of challenges, including complaints from parents about the homework load that he was giving to students. It caused him to have a lot of anxiety and low self-esteem. But he learned a lot that first year of teaching. Soon, Alexander had to do a performance evaluation, which consisted of multiple observations from the principal to his class. Alexander was nervous and anxious about this entire process, but he prepared as best as he could. He spent ten hours preparing his lesson plans, so they would be perfect and would display his competence in teaching. He practiced with a camera and in front of the mirror at home. He wanted to do his best job for this evaluation. When it came time for his evaluation, Alex was very nervous about it. He could hardly move the day of it. He had not slept well the previous night. But once he got to his class, he did a lot better. During the class, he focused on delivering the lesson according to his plan. Everything went well and in the end, his principal praised him for doing a great job on his evaluation. He finally was able to get a raise on his salary, which made him feel really good.

As you can see, there are several main emotions to deal with while developing your career: envy, frustration, and anxiety. But these emotions can be dealt with constructively to foster positive feelings. When you can focus on how to leverage your emotions, then you can manage the difficult situations you might find in the workplace. It can be uncomfortable to work on your career and develop your professional profile. You cannot always avoid difficult emotions and experiences. However, you can have a proactive perspective that is positive and willing to grow from everything that you have to go through in your career. There are always ups and downs that we have to experience, but once we have endured it for a period of time, we feel more resilient and able to handle all the challenges we face. That makes us stronger and more competent as professionals.

Chapter 11: Emotional Regulation and Mental Health

In this chapter, we are going to talk about how to regulate your emotions and contribute to better mental health. We have already discussed the topic of depression and anxiety. Now, we can talk about how important it is to raise awareness about mental health.

Mental health in America is in crisis. There are so many reasons that people are depressed, anxious, or worried. Many people are hiding behind closed doors, unwilling to disclose mental illness or any other matters in their lives. Consequently, we have people who are sicker than ever and absent from work more often. School children are struggling, because they are dealing with depression and they don't have anyone to go to for support. That is where we have to find ways to raise awareness for mental health and enable people to get the treatment they need.

Why Mental Health is Important for Emotional Regulation

Many of the mental illnesses a person can have are caused by emotional dysfunction. As a result, they require us to treat the problems within a person. They are also psychological, so the brain is the key instrument in the regulation of emotions. When the emotions are out of control, then a person may fly off the handle and do things they wouldn't normally do. They might become depressed and want to spend a lot of time in bed. Or, they might react violently, in a manic way, or abnormally. Then, they will need to seek treatment for their condition. In today's world, it is important that we encourage people to get help when it is needed. It is vital that people are aware of the support systems available to get them on the right track.

Mental Health Treatment Options

It would seem counterintuitive to encourage someone to seek treatment from a professional, but this is exactly what needs to be done. More people need to see doctors and therapists about their problems. These medical professionals can diagnose and treat patients with a variety of health issues. They can also refer people to specialists, so they can get specific help for their condition. Many mental health issues are left undiagnosed and therefore untreated. This causes many problems for society, including people hurting others or even taking their own lives.

The need to treat mental illness has never been greater than now. Therefore, it is crucial for us to find ways we can remove the stigma of it, so that people feel less ashamed of their condition and more willing to seek help. Too many people carry with them a great deal of shame and guilt attached to their mental illness. That causes them to be unable to function. They are more absent from work, feel the need to isolate themselves, and are much unhealthier. When people can become part of a community, they are more willing to share their struggles and difficulties. That is why it is important to join some kind of community, whether that is with a church or other nonprofit organizations.

The Impact of Mental Health on Wellness

Taking care of mental health is an important part of emotional regulation, because when we can help people take care of their mental health needs, then we can bring them to a point of wellness. It takes a bit of proactivity and awareness, but once we do that, we will bring everything to light. Then, we can create a positive impact on mental health. People will become well and experience freedom like none other. Mental health is an important issue in today's society. We shouldn't allow opportunities to pass to give people encouragement and support, because the world needs that. We need to offer people the chance to get well and seek help, because then, they can manage their emotions well and live full and meaningful lives.

Case Study

Jaric was diagnosed with anxiety disorder when he was seventeen years old. He had experienced panic attacks in his life more than three times. He was finally admitted to the hospital one day after attempting to take his own life. Jaric had to spend time in the hospital. It was not easy for him, but he knew that he had to do it. He received a variety of antipsychotic medications that had side effects. His doctor told him that he would need to take this medication for a while. At first, he was resistant to the idea. Then, he felt that needed to do it to stay well. Jaric's parents and teachers were supportive and helped him get back to where he needed to be. They helped him get through his senior year and complete his schoolwork, so he could graduate from high school. It was not an easy time. There were struggles, and Jaric had difficulty staying motivated. Slowly but surely, he got better and felt that he could complete his senior year and stay well. Jaric felt isolated from his friends because he was always dealing with his anxiety, but he felt that he could overcome his condition and that he could have a meaningful life. Jaric's doctor told him that he could live a normal life if he simply complied and did all the treatment and psychotherapy. To this day, Jaric has been well and has dealt with limited cases of anxiety all because he was proactive in getting the treatment for his condition. He was successful in managing his mental illness and could live a full and normal life.

To sum up, it is crucial to be aware of mental health issues and how they affect people. Mental illness continues to be a problem that plagues the American public. As long as we keep people hiding in their houses, we will not address the problems of mental illness and emotional regulation. As we raise awareness and invite people into the light of recovery and vulnerability, we give people the chance to thrive and succeed in their lives. We offer them the opportunity to make the most of their lives and experience breakthroughs like no other. Let's encourage people to get help and live life to the fullest.

Chapter 12:
Maintaining Wellness Every Day

The final chapter of this book will talk about how to maintain wellness in your life, which helps to improve your emotional state. We all need to know how to be well and live a good life. Having healthy habits is one of the most important ways to be emotionally stable. When we live a healthy lifestyle, then we can feel that we are at our best and optimum state. Let's look at some healthy habits that we can follow as we are maintaining wellness.

Sleep Well at Night

Sleep is one of the most important and yet often neglected aspects of our lives. More people are going without sleep than ever before. Part of the reason is that we don't prioritize it, but also, we don't make time for it. With our hectic schedules, we don't place importance on getting enough sleep at night. But it has been proven that we need our sleep to live a healthy and balanced lifestyle. We should get at least 7-9 hours of sleep per night, so we can have a productive day. Sleeping is an important part of wellness, because we spent over a third of our lives in bed.

Sleep is important not only to our physical health but also to our emotional well-being. When we get enough sleep at night, we feel better about ourselves and our situation. Often, a lack of sleep will cause us to feel grumpy, sleepy, and unable to function the next day. It causes us to go heavy on the caffeine and drink too much coffee and soda. Then, we have a variety of other health problems. In addition, sleep deprivation leads to illness and absenteeism from work. It can also lead to burnout in the workplace and at school. So, don't ever think you need to stay up all night to do things. Get some sleep. Your emotions and mental health will thank you.

Exercise Often

Another thing that is often neglected in our busy schedule is exercise, but it is one of the most crucial aspects of our lives. We need to get more exercise. With more Americans overweight and sedentary, there is no wonder that so many people are out of shape and unable to do things in their lives. Exercising can be fun, and it releases a lot of feel-good chemicals, which make us experience more positive emotions.

What kinds of exercises can you do? There are many options available. You can run on the treadmill, swim in the pool, play basketball, or simply walk around the block. The main thing is to find something that suits you. Everyone is different. Not everyone is cut out to go to the gym. Some people prefer to do things on their own, while others like to do team sports. Each person has their own preference, and there is no right or wrong answer to this question. Therefore, find an activity that you enjoy and do it regularly. You won't regret it for a second. When you find exercises you love to do, you will feel the difference in both your body and mind.

Exercise can help us feel better about ourselves. It increases our self-confidence and enables us to be better people. We can leverage a variety of positive emotions when we feel healthy. Therefore, we should find ways to exercise regularly and experience the freedom that comes from living a better lifestyle.

When we exercise, we can also manage our weight and lose the excess pounds and belly fat that cause us trouble and make us feel bad about ourselves and self-image. We can be more active and feel healthier, as a result. Find an exercise that is right for you and you will have a wellness routine that provides great benefits.

Eat a Balanced Diet

Another thing that many people struggle with is their diet. They eat unhealthy junk food or eat too big of portions. Keep in mind that American portions are excessive and that many people struggle with this and often eat more than they should. When you eat a balanced diet, you can feel better about yourself, because you'll be eating right. You eat more fruits and vegetables and lean meat, which promotes a healthier lifestyle. In addition, you become less prone to illness.

When you eat a balanced diet, you will feel much better about your life. You will be able to manage your weight and feel more confident about your self-image. It will promote a lot of positive emotions. In general, your mental and physical health will receive a boost of energy.

Avoid Smoking or Excessive Drinking

In addition to sleeping, diet, and exercise, we should cultivate good habits that promote a healthy lifestyle. Unfortunately, many people revert to negative coping mechanisms to provide stress relief, such as nicotine or alcohol. Smoking is still the leading preventable cause of death in the United States. People continue to light up even after receiving so many health warnings. It is time to quit today. If you are a smoker, you should find ways to get stress relief not through cigarettes. Find a healthier habit to follow each day and you will feel the difference. Your body will feel better and you will also have a better time sleeping at night. Nicotine affects sleep cycles, which causes you to experience insomnia and sleeplessness. In addition, cigarette smoke has many carcinogens, which are not good for your heart and lungs and can cause a variety of health problems both in the short-term and long-term. There are many consequences that you must deal with when continuing to smoke. You have to weight those consequences and decide what you need to do. But the best decision is to quit cold turkey and simply not do it anymore.

Excessive drinking is a problem that continues to be an issue for people. Families get ripped apart from alcoholism and many people get liver cancer and other diseases as a result of excessive drinking. Especially among the younger generation, drinking has become a thing that many people regularly engage in to cope with stress. Drunkenness, however, can cause people to be out of control and experience things that are simply not healthy. It can cause sleeplessness and addiction that feed into every aspect of a person's life. In addition, it can cause a wide variety of emotional problems, including depression. Alcohol has a potent impact on our health and we would do well to avoid too much of it. Although alcohol can be consumed in moderate amounts that do not have any consequences to health, many people abuse it and should abstain from it for a while. Some people can control themselves and the amount of alcohol they can take in, while others cannot control themselves. Each person should recognize the amount of alcohol they can readily take in before getting drunk, so they can avoid drinking too much. That is a very individual decision. Be wise and do what is right for you.

Managing Time and Avoiding Procrastination

Many people struggle with time management. They are unable to manage their own time and therefore cannot keep up with the various situations in which they find themselves. In addition, many people procrastinate too much, because they put off unappealing tasks and do them later, right before they are due, creating a burden of stress and anxiety. When we learn to manage our stress and avoid procrastination, then we allow ourselves to be free of anxiety. We feel less stressed or nervous about the future. We can be in total control over our time and then we don't have to worry about anything. Instead, we find time for all the things we need to do.

Managing time will require patience and perseverance. But once you have it down, then you will find that you can "make" time for all the things you need to in your schedule. You understand the importance of prioritizing and you make sure to allot the correct amount of time for each task. Then, you feel less stressed and burdened by things. It will make your life a lot easier and more productive.

Having a Positive Social Life

In addition to all these healthy habits, we also need the help of other people. Support through social life enables us to connect with those around us and find ways of having a good lifestyle. It is important for us to have friends and workmates we can connect with and have a good time with. Often, our emotions can be controlled and managed when we have other people in our lives, who can be good influences and help us to be happier. With social isolation becoming a greater problem, more people are lonelier than ever. Even with social media and "connections" online, we still find ourselves hiding behind a screen and revealing parts of our lives, but not the whole story. Therefore, the need for human connection in real-time is one of the most important parts of our lives. We need to be experiencing our lives "here and now," not in a virtual world. However, too many people are struggling to do that, because they are slaves to technology. When you can surround yourself with good people, who can encourage and support you, then you will feel a lot healthier and more able to deal with issues such as depression and anxiety. When you have a friend to call when you're feeling down, you will feel you can keep going and live your life in spite of hardship. People with supportive friends tend to live longer and become more resilient to challenges in their lives. Therefore, we need to find friends, who can help us to live meaningful and happy lives.

Disconnecting from Technology

Related to the issue of connectedness is the problem of technology. While our smartphones, the internet, and other technologies have greatly enhanced our lives, they have also caused us to become enslaved to our devices. Technology has made us more reliant on external devices to support us. Smartphone addiction is widespread throughout the world, as more people buy these phones. Technology can make us very unhappy, because we are constantly living in the virtual world but not enough in real-life. Consequently, we feel the need to always be "connected" to everyone in the world. The positive thing is that we can talk to anyone in the world at any time, because we have technology and the internet. The world is more connected than ever before, but social isolation continues to be a huge issue.

One of the ways we can get rid of this problem is to disconnect from technology. You see many people trying to live a balanced life by getting rid of their smartphones, deactivating their Facebook and Instagram accounts, and other things. These are all good ways to disconnect and find ways to do some soul-searching. We need time away from our devices. We cannot always use them. When we go on technology retreats or disconnect from the outside world, it can be a scary thing. But it is worth it for our emotional and mental wellbeing. So, find a day or two where you can get away from the Internet or smartphone. You can start to re-evaluate your time and investment. It will help you experience freedom like no other.

How Do These Habits Promote Emotional Well-Being?

You might be wondering; how do all these habits promote emotional well-being. Well, just living a healthy lifestyle is enough to make you feel better. When you live an unhealthy lifestyle with bad eating habits, smoking, drinking, sleep deprivation, among other things, you're setting up yourself to a life devoid of happiness. You will feel bad about yourself, your circumstances, and sometimes the people around you. It will not help you feel emotionally stable. Your moods will go up and down because you're dependent on sugar, nicotine, or alcohol for your happiness. But when you can cultivate positive and healthy habits, you will feel more emotionally grounded. You won't waver and experience waves of emotion. Instead, you will be completely stable most of the time. Granted, you may not always feel amazing, but you can feel happier and more secure, because you are in a place of emotional maturity, which can handle anything. If you're searching for something in your life, you should seek after emotional stability. By following these healthy habits, you will feel that your emotions stay in one place. You will feel happy and healthy, which is what everyone needs to feel in their lives. Let's now close with an example of a healthy lifestyle.

Case Study

Joey engaged in a lot of bad habits in his twenties. He smoked sixty cigarettes a day and would drink lots of beer on the weekends. He could also get drunk and have massive hangovers every Saturday. Joey also began to gain weight and had a beer belly. His addiction to gaming and clubbing caused him to have a lot of health problems. Sometimes, he would even get sick from all this social interaction. Once he had heart palpitations and had to go to the hospital after drinking too much. When this happened, Joey had a near-death experience. He had to go through rehab for three months in a facility near his home. During that time, he received a lot of help for his condition. People told him he needed to modify his diet and eat less carbs. He stopped alcohol cold turkey and never drank another beer again. He also cut down on smoking cigarettes and made a plan to completely quit after a while. Eventually, he started to go to the gym. Instead of going clubbing on a Saturday night, he would exercise on the treadmill and meet his gym-mates, who could encourage and support him. All in all, he felt like he was getting along fine. Things were improving. Eventually, Joey had a healthy lifestyle and he spoke to youth about it at different conferences. He highlighted his journey to recovery and clearly illustrated how he had been led through that time to recover from his addictions. It was an amazing testimony. He felt that he was healing from that time of his life and felt he could handle anything that came his way. In the end, Joey could handle his emotions and became healthier. He was truly happy.

It is important to see that healthy habits form the person. Unhealthy habits have the power to destroy us. They can rob us of all the joy and meaning in our lives and turn us into miserable people. But once we accept that we can change our habits, then we can live a life that is filled with happiness and peace. By making the effort to change our habits, we can experience breakthroughs that will promote our overall health and recovery. It takes a lot of time to make these changes, but little by little, we can change and develop into people, who can leverage more positive emotions. Then, we can encourage others to do the same, like Joey. If you want to live a happier and more stable emotional life, find ways to live a healthy lifestyle. Sleep well, eat a balanced diet, avoid smoking and drinking, get your exercise, manage your time, and limit your use of technology. If you follow through these guidelines, we guarantee you will experience amazing results. You will live the life you were meant to lead.

Conclusion

Emotional intelligence is something that we develop our whole lives. It starts when we are young and in school. We develop an emotional intelligence over time. For some, it is a bit slower than others. Over our lifetime, we develop our ability to relate to our emotions. As we age, emotions become less overpowering, as we find ways to cope with them. Nevertheless, they can be forces that can carry us away, if we are not careful.

This book has been intended to introduce you to emotional intelligence. We walked you through how to develop your EQ, how EQ is learned from childhood to adulthood, how to be a powerful influence at work with your EQ, and also the ways of coping with negative emotions. With the information in this book, you will be able to change the world by applying the principles of emotional intelligence. You will understand more about how people work and how their emotional sensitivity makes them who they are. You will also be more empathic toward others. It is an amazing thing.

As you go about your life, you recognize how much emotions can take over your life. They are difficult to overcome, especially when we feel anxious, depressed, or worried. We feel as if the world is ending before our eyes when we have a crisis. Once we have mastered the difficult emotions in our lives, then nothing will faze us again. We will be calm under pressure and able to face the problems in our lives. No more need to overreact to situations. We hope that you have found this information helpful to overcoming the difficult emotions in your life. Through our case studies based on real-life examples and adapted for this book, we have shown you how it really works. You can have emotional intelligence and influence the world around you.

Thank you for joining us on this journey into emotional intelligence. Having read this book, we know that you will be more informed and ready to influence a generation by boosting their emotional intelligence. It is powerful. For a better future, a higher EQ!

References

Brodwin, E. and Gould, S. (2017). When Your Brain Matures at Everything--it isn't even fully developed until the age of 25. Business Insider. Retrieved from https://www.businessinsider.com/age-brain-matures-at-everything-2017-11

Cherry, K. (2018). The 6 Types of Basic Emotions and Their Effect on Human Behavior. Verywellmind. Retrieved from https://www.verywellmind.com/an-overview-of-the-types-of-emotions-4163976

Cherry, K. (2019). An Overview of Emotional Intelligence. Verywellmind. Retrieved from https://www.verywellmind.com/what-is-emotional-intelligence-2795423

Cherry, K. (2019). Social and Emotional Development in Early Childhood. Verywellmind. Retrieved from https://www.verywellmind.com/social-and-emotional-development-in-early-childhood-2795106

Cudmore, D. (n.d.) Emotional Intelligence. Is It Why You Didn't Get the Promotion? Digital.com. Retrieved from https://digital.com/blog/emotional-intelligence/

Mental Health Days: How Teens Changed the Law in Oregon (2019). BBC News. Retrieved from https://www.bbc.com/news/newsbeat-49070822?ns_mchannel=social&ns_source=facebook&ns_campaign=bbcnews&ocid=socialflow_facebook&fbclid=IwAR23Bt5IJ1cFYx0EClod5kYbNhQ291lpbjz7QiZPW_901dxHpt_QHplbTv8

Salazar, A. (2017). Emotional Intelligence: What is it, interpretation models and controversies. CogniFit. Retrieved from https://blog.cognifit.com/emotional-intelligence/

www.ingramcontent.com/pod-product-compliance
Lightning Source LLC
Chambersburg PA
CBHW030158100526
44592CB00009B/332